What Is a Wave?

Linda Ivancic

Cavendish
Square

New York

Published in 2016 by Cavendish Square Publishing, LLC
243 5th Avenue, Suite 136, New York, NY 10016

Website: cavendishsq.com

This publication represents the opinions and views of the author based on his or her personal experience, knowledge, and research. The information in this book serves as a general guide only. The author and publisher have used their best efforts in preparing this book and disclaim liability rising directly or indirectly from the use and application of this book.

CPSIA Compliance Information: Batch #CW16CSQ

All websites were available and accurate when this book was sent to press.

Library of Congress Cataloging-in-Publication Data

Ivancic, Linda, author.
What is a wave? / Linda Ivancic.
pages cm – (Unseen science)
Includes index.
ISBN 978-1-5026-0918-2 (hardcover) ISBN 978-1-5026-0917-5 (paperback) ISBN 978-1-5026-0919-9 (ebook)
1. Waves—Juvenile literature. 2. Wave mechanics—Juvenile literature. I. Title. II. Series: Unseen science.
QC157.I93 2016
531'.1133—dc23

2015022176

Editorial Director: David McNamara
Editor: Andrew Coddington
Copy Editor: Rebecca Rohan
Art Director: Jeffrey Talbot
Designer: Joseph Macri/Amy Greenan
Senior Production Manager: Jennifer Ryder-Talbot
Production Editor: Renni Johnson
Photo Research: J8 Media

Printed in the United States of America

CONTENTS

CHAPTER 1

Waves Everywhere

Do you see waves? Do you hear waves? Do you feel waves? The answer to all three questions is yes! Waves are present all around us. Some waves we can see, such as waves on a lake or the ocean.

Other waves we hear, when they bring sound to our eardrums as we listen to our favorite music.

There are even waves at work when we feel the earth move during an earthquake.

There are other waves that we can't see, but they act on cold food to cook it or make it hot when we use the **microwave** oven!

Waves on water are visible waves formed mainly by the wind.

The force of waves can cause great damage.

Waves vibrate our eardrums so we can hear.

Many waves, such as microwaves, cannot be seen.

Waves are everywhere! There are many jobs that a wave can do. But all waves, whether we see, hear, or feel them, have one thing in common—they all **transfer**, or move, energy. A wave moves through a material like water, air, earth, or food. When we talk about the experience of a wave, we are really looking at how energy is transferred.

So Really, What Is a Wave?

If a wave moves or transports energy in each of the everyday examples we just shared, then all waves must have some things in common, no matter what they do. Before we can talk about each of these different and special types of waves, let's take a look at how we observe and describe the features that all waves share.

Properties of a Wave

Have you ever watched the waves on a lake or the ocean? They look a little like the drawing (*right*). To describe a wave, scientists draw it on a **graph**. The graph is used by scientists to show and describe what the wave looks like using scientific terms. A graph of a wave is also like a photo of a friend, in that we are only seeing a wave at a moment in time.

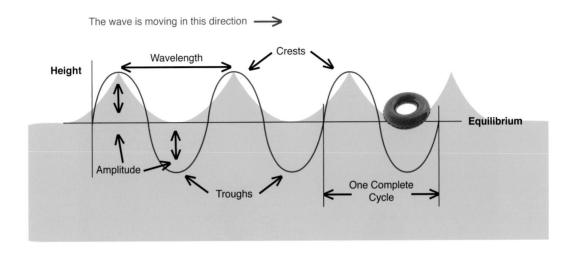

Scientists explain waves using the following terms: **crest**, **trough**, **equilibrium**, **amplitude**, **wavelength**, and **frequency**.

A wave graph is drawn on a chart where the vertical (up and down) axis shows the height of the wave and the horizontal (sideways) axis shows either distance or time.

The highest point of the wave is called the crest and the lowest point is called the trough. The imaginary line through the center of the wave graph is the resting position showing the ocean surface (in our example) as if there were no wave. This is also called the equilibrium.

Look at the waves. Can you see the crest, trough and resting position? Where is the raft located?

Walking is easy in these low-energy waves.

What Is a Wave?

Wavelength

The wavelength of a wave is the measure of the distance between two matching points of a wave. This can be measured between two crests of a wave or two troughs of a wave.

Amplitude

The amplitude of a wave is a measure of the height (or depth) of the wave from its equilibrium position. The amplitude tells us about the strength of a wave. Together, wavelength and amplitude show the power and strength of a wave. If you were walking in the water along the beach and saw the ocean waves lapping slowly and gently at your ankles, we would say that the wavelength is long. The amplitude is short. These are weak waves.

On the other hand, if we were bodysurfing in the water, we would get maximum enjoyment out of waves that were high and moved quickly toward shore. Waves with a short wavelength and high amplitude can be a lot of fun!

Frequency

The frequency of a wave is the number of times a wave cycles, or passes through something (like the air, water, or soil), in an amount of time. Frequency tells us the rate or how often. Frequency is usually measured in a unit called a **hertz** (shown as Hz). One hertz equals one cycle per second. While sitting on the beach after our day of fun in the water, we could observe how often the ocean waves hit the pier in one minute.

This Chapter Has Shown

So far we have read that there are different kinds of waves present in the world around us, some of which we are not able to see. Waves transfer sound, light, and seismic energy. All waves have crests, troughs, wavelength, and frequency. These characteristics are used to describe and measure waves.

Waves contain unique characteristics that are in action all around us.

CHAPTER 2

Surf's Up!

We have talked about where we find waves. We have talked about different parts of a wave. We have seen what a wave looks like when it is drawn on a graph. Now, let's make a wave!

Show Me

Objective

To make and observe the characteristics of a wave.

Materials

- One pan with a rim; it needs to be able to hold water
- One large spoon, either metal or plastic
- One paper cupcake liner, a plastic bottle cap, or a cork

Bodysurfing on the water is a fun way to use waves!

Procedure

1. Find a place to do the experiment. Water may spill, so choose a space where water will not cause damage or injury.

2. Place your pan on a flat surface like a countertop or a table.

3. Using another container, get water and fill the pan so that it is about half-full when you look at the water level along the inside the pan.

Your pan and spoon should be set up like this.

What Is a Wave?

4. Carefully and slowly lift one end of the pan just high enough to place the large spoon upside down under the end of the pan, as shown in the photo (*left*). If water spills over the edge, use the container to scoop out some water.
5. Now you are ready to make a wave! Quickly pull out the spoon from under the pan.
6. Observe the water. Watch the water level along the inside of the pan.

Questions

- What formed in the water?
- How did the water move in the pan?
- Can you see and name the parts of a wave?

Now, repeat the procedure, but this time before pulling out the spoon, place the paper liner (or bottle cap) in the center of the pan filled with water.

Questions

- Did the water do anything different?
- What did the liner do?

Make another wave and observe what happens to the paper liner.

You can use a ruler to measure how far the liner traveled, and to measure the amplitude or height of the wave.

You can also use a watch or clock to record the time in seconds for the wave to travel from one end of the pan to the other. Try to determine the time it takes for the wave to travel through a full cycle, from when you pulled out the spoon to when the wave comes back to the starting point.

Did You Know?

The science that deals with matter, energy, motion, and force is called **physics**.

Conclusion

In the experiment, energy introduced into the water formed a visible wave in which you observed its crest and equilibrium. You were also able to see the energy of the wave carrying the paper liner. As the wave traveled, it lost energy and disappeared over time.

CHAPTER 3

Not All Waves Are the Same

Waves are present all around us in nature, such as the waves we see on the ocean. Waves are also at work when we hear music, a screaming baby sister, or an alarm clock; when we feel the earth move during an earthquake; or when we heat up cold food using the microwave oven. The special types of waves that make these familiar things happen are **sound waves**, **seismic waves**, and microwaves.

Sound waves carry vibrations and can be pleasant to hear.

Sound Waves

A wave is defined as a transfer of energy from one point to another. We can understand how sound happens by studying the movement of sound waves. Sound is a wave that is created when an object vibrates. This vibration travels from its source to another location. Usually sound waves travel through air, but they can also travel through other substances like metal or water.

Some sounds we don't want to hear!

Did you know that sound waves can travel at a speed of 1,115 feet (340 meters) per second?

Sound waves are produced by many things, including the plucking of a guitar string, the clanging of a spoon against a glass, and using your voice to speak!

The energy in the sound we make progresses through the air (or water or metal) by **particle**-to-particle interaction. To hear the sound of that guitar string, first a particle of air near the string is moved from its resting equilibrium. That particle pushes into a neighboring particle, and continues pushing into other air particles

What Is a Wave?

If we nudged the first child, we would see energy transferred between the children in the form of a mechanical wave.

along the way. Eventually, the vibration from the guitar string is received by the eardrum. Because the sound energy is transferred from one particle to another, the particle-to-particle transfer process is called a **mechanical wave**.

All waves are measured using frequencies. Our human hearing can detect sound waves that have frequencies between 20 Hz and 20,000 Hz. There are sound waves that only animals can hear, called **infrasound**, with frequencies below 20 Hz, and **ultrasound** waves, with frequencies above 20,000 Hz.

Ultrasound waves are used in the medical field. Instead of performing surgery to look inside the body, this type of sound wave can travel through the skin and back to a sensor to detect and measure an object within the body. These objects may include organs, tumors, and even babies growing inside their mothers.

In the field of engineering, ultrasound waves have been used to map the surface of the ocean floor and test the strength of manufactured goods. Ultrasound waves are also used to locate airplane crashes or ships lost at sea.

Seismic Waves

In many parts of the United States and other places around the world, earthquakes are common. A seismic wave is formed when the energy from an earthquake travels within the earth or along its surface. Earthquakes are the most common source of the energy but explosions can also generate these waves. A **seismograph** is used to detect the energy traveling in these waves and to measure their size. The size of the waves is called the magnitude. Earthquakes are rated on the Richter scale to indicate their intensity.

There are two types of seismic waves: body waves and surface waves. Body waves move energy through the inner layers (or body)

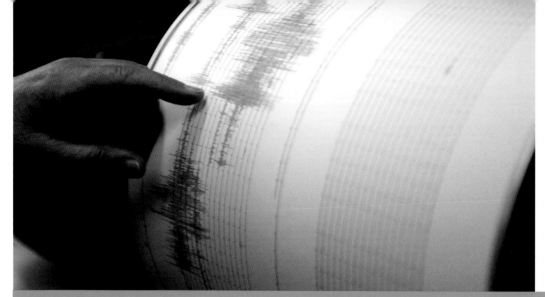

This recording of seismic waves on the seismograph looks similar to the wave graph we saw in Chapter 1.

of the earth and arrive at a given point before surface waves. These waves have a higher frequency than surface waves. Like sound waves, these waves push and pull nearby particles, but instead of air, they move solid rock. Because of this, they are called **compressional waves**. There are two types of body waves. These are based on what type of earth material they move through and how the particles react when moved by the energy.

Surface waves only move along the earth's surface, almost like waves on a lake. Surface waves cause a rolling or swaying motion of the earth. These waves have a lower frequency. As surface waves carry their energy near the ground's surface, the energy is transferred to things like buildings, roads, sewers, and power lines. Since we live in buildings, travel on roads to go places, and use water and electricity every day, damage from an earthquake can be devastating to a community.

Understanding the energy in seismic waves and how they influence the movement of the earth is an important task for engineers and planners. In areas where earthquakes happen often engineers must choose building materials that are strong or even bendable so that buildings are stable and safe.

The energy from seismic waves is very powerful.

Architects use science to design buildings that can withstand earthquakes.

This Chapter Has Shown

There are many types of waves. Sound is a wave that is created when an object vibrates, or shakes. Sound waves move through air, water, or metal. One type of sound wave is ultrasound. Scientists and doctors use ultrasound to "see" through things. Seismic waves are formed when the energy from an earthquake or explosions travels through the earth. Studying the energy of seismic waves allows engineers to build safer buildings, roads, and utility systems.

GLOSSARY

amplitude The measure of the displacement of the wave from its rest position.

compressional waves A wave, like a sound wave, in which energy travels through particle-to-particle transfer across a material such as rock.

crest The highest point of a wave form.

equilibrium The resting point of a wave where no energy is passing through.

frequency The rate something happens over a time period or the rate at which a wave is measured, usually per second.

graph A diagram showing the relationship between two or more things.

hertz The measurement of how often something occurs per one second interval, usually written as Hz.

infrasound Sound frequencies that fall below 20 Hz, and are not heard by humans.

mechanical wave A wave that moves its energy through a material (air, water, soil) as in sound waves and water waves.

microwave An electromagnetic wave with a frequency between that of infrared and radio waves. Microwaves are used in radar, cooking, and other applications.

particle A very small piece, or the smallest possible amount of something.

physics The science that deals with matter, energy, motion and force.

seismic waves The energy caused by the movement of rock in the earth or by an explosion.

seismograph The device used to detect and measure the energy of seismic waves.

GLOSSARY

sound waves A vibration transported by particle-to-particle through a material. It is characterized as a mechanical wave.

transfer The act of moving something to another place.

trough The lowest point of a wave.

ultrasound A sound wave with a frequency greater than the upper threshold of human frequency, that is greater than 20,000 Hz.

wavelength The measure of the distance between two matching points of a wave, such as the crest or trough.

Books

Johnson, Robin. *How Does Sound Change?* New York, NY: Crabtree Publishing Company, 2014.

Winchester, Simon. *When the Earth Shakes: Earthquakes, Volcanoes, and Tsunamis*. New York, NY: Penguin Young Readers Group, 2015

Websites

ASPIRE (Astrophysics Science Project Integrating Research and Education)

aspire.cosmic-ray.org/Labs/WaveBasics/waves.htm
This site defines and shows through animation the interrelationships between frequency, wavelength, and amplitude.

HowStuffWorks.com

science.howstuffworks.com/nature/natural-disasters/earthquake4.htm

This site shows and explains how energy is generated in an earthquake and explains the characteristics of seismic waves.

PhysicsClassroom.com

www.physicsclassroom.com/Physics-Interactives/Waves-and-Sound/Simple-Wave-Simulator/Simple-Wave-Simulator-Interactive

This interactive feature shows various wave properties and how they are affected when the characteristics of a wave are changed.

INDEX

Page numbers in **boldface** are illustrations. Entries in **boldface** are glossary terms.

ABOUT THE AUTHOR

Linda Ivancic's love for the natural world comes from when her mother told her to "Go outside and play!" Waves were part of her everyday life growing up near Lake Ontario. She comes to writing children's books after twenty-eight years as an environmental, health and safety consultant. She has visited and explored many fascinating places around the world, always learning something new. Motivated by her adult learners' "ah-ha" moments when they grasp science in the world around them, she is committed to making science interesting and approachable to all age groups. Linda enjoys singing and "playing outside" where you will find her exploring on her bike, at the lake, and in the woods.